A WILLOW GROWS
ASLANT A BROOK

A WILLOW GROWS ASLANT A BROOK

POEMS

AARON CHASE EDDINGTON

Bowen Press

—— TYLER, TEXAS ——

Published 2020 by
Bowen Press
Tyler, TX 75703
BowenPressBooks.com

ISBN 978-0-578-65243-6

Printed in the United States of America

CONTENTS

Art is a curious command. We must do what we are bidden to do and can go only so far as the light permits. I am always earnest as you, if anyone, must know. But no doubt I puzzle you—as I do myself.

—WILLIAM CARLOS WILLIAMS

VERMEER DREAMED OF YOU LOADING
THE DISHWASHER

A corona of evening light haloed through
the kitchen windows
illuminating the soft contours of your cheek and chin
your hair, painted golden red as the sunset, pulled up
into a bun messy and frenetic
your night shirt draped
loosely from your shoulders
and still you wore those yellow gloves
that never quite managed to
keep your hands from pruning
while you rinsed the dishes.

Afterward you took them off and called out
to come kiss your candied apricot fingers
but no one came
before he awoke.

ODE ON A KINTSUGI URN

Truth, beauty enough exists in the
    marbled glaze, its
iridescent rusts and blues dance on the
    lacquered
surface, the curved stoneware a timeless
    form, yet here
is a fissure, a fault-line where it all fell
    apart, traced by
ribbons of gold, spiderwebbing along its
    length, the seam
restored, and it seems something more
    than beauty endures
in the cold broken thing, in the fracture
    healed, but still,
O urn what holy dust spilled from you
    when you fell—
what sacred ash scattered as you broke
    upon the earth? No,
just tell me how your golden scars made
    you whole again.

WHEN THOU CUTTEST DOWN THINE HARVEST

The spring my father passed
he set me loose in the woods
to play with the chickens
that scratched for their meals
in the fractured light scattered
against the forest floor;

through the pines I saw him
in the clearing, as his brown, sinewy
arms guided the mechanized tiller
down the plotted row, his breast
pockets swelling with seeds that,
in time, he would drop into the furrows;

much later, we other men stooped
in his garden to shear away
the peppers, cucumber, and okra—
careful not to squander the harvest
that he planted but
could not reap.

DEODAND

For Oscar Alberto Martínez Ramírez and his daughter,
Valeria

it had been many weeks, barefoot,
or nearly so and your shoulders ached
from the burden of the turtle-shelled life
clinging to your back, quietly desperate,
and so hungry that she didn't even cry anymore,
but you went together the whole way—
did you sing old *boleros* across the desert
before you came to the water, did you fall
to your knees and drink, choking it down
the wrong pipe, coughing, swimming, bleary-
eyed and hopeful? Tossed by the water, the currents
of Nature kidnapped the fragile child from your back,
and still you swam after her, thrown by the wake, your
muscles must have burned hot, as though running in a
    dream;

they found you days later, your skin bloated
white as the meat of an apple, your arms wrapped
closely around the thing you could not lose, and
so, the trade you made to hold her—fair enough—
was to sink your hope into murky water, offered as
a sacrifice to the big river, running wide,
hungry for more

MIRACLE*

For Jason

Not the miracle of the girl who got up from
     her rest
but the one of her father who felt not afraid
who, silent, caressed her sweat-slicked hair
     with hands,
sun-tanned and calloused, quieting her
     violent fever dream.

It was here that the father watched his
     daughter dying;
in a moment beyond hope, beyond grief, his
     chest heavy,
jaw tight, he resolved to find the Healer, and
     went, leaving
behind him the others who gnashed and
     wailed at the walls.

* Adapted from Seamus Heaney's poem of the same name that originally
appeared in his collection *Human Chain*.

SEWING A BUTTON ONTO YOUR
FAVORITE BLOUSE

The line split in the eye
when you tried to thread the needle,
and the spool unraveled into your lap, so

you left it, you abandoned
the tangled vine of purple thread that
buffeted across the countertop

by the slow spinning ceiling fan
while you went searching for
something else to wear.

AGONY IN THE GARDEN

Once I was as thin as a barrel stave.
During the times I ill afforded regular suppers,
I would instead walk to Ashland to forget
my hunger among the blooming flowers—

on a mischievous night, I climbed over
the brick walls with my girl, and dropped
down into Henry Clay's English garden where
she kissed me by the lilies of the valley;

it was fully night before we clambered
back out, to stroll the wood-chipped paths
under fat-bellied Antebellum oaks, their
wide branches canopying the whole estate,

and us, alone, beneath them—
we were evangelists of the flesh
professing, briefly,
holiness in all things.

FORESHADOWS

From the top deck I heard the
low wailing howl in the distant ocean and

said nothing, not even *look—there*
as you stood by me (did you hear it, too?)

and then came the plaintive echoes
from the calving as the berg

tumbled into the sea.

FIELD'S NOCTURNE NO. 1 IN E FLAT MAJOR

The music played in half-time
while you taught me
to dance—

we'd dragged the chairs
to the corners of the den
rolled the rug away

so that we'd have space
for a sweeping box-step
across the hardwood floor;

but you resisted when I
pulled you closer, smiled and
asked you to ignore

the buzzing
phone
on the table.

A MEMORY OF OKLAHOMA

We boys lied
supine and naked
in the river
floating, spitting
fountains of red water

while the others
sat on ice chests
drinking grape soda
and smoking cigarettes;

each of us, in our way,
looked past the cloudless sky
before loading into the car
on our way
to the next state.

STILL LIFE, NO. 1

On my bedside table
a lowball glass of water from the tap and a
gold watch with a salt-stained leather strap atop
Heaney, Hughes, *A Handful of Dust*

ARRIVING

For Wendell Berry and his poem "Going"

Like a man drunk in sleep, darkened,
the body resists the light.
Somersaulted, it writhes as the eye and
the mind stay turned from the world.

But a force stronger than force compels
life, pushes the unforgiving thing to,
irresistibly, until one by one
its faculties awaken
crying and wriggling free
like a movement beyond revolution,
suddenly knowing—until it is
like the thrush singing at dawn;
it animates the morning and calls
life into life, love into love.

And finally, the mind, the eyes too,
birthed to know, to become, to see,
arrive.

WOMAN IN CHIAROSCURO

A specter haunts my house.
It follows me, or precedes me,
through the empty rooms;
at night it lies heavy on my chest, or

leaves its imprint in the space beside me, so
I spend the evenings out, despairing, but still
I feel the dusky fetid breath on my neck
when I return, standing beneath the portico

anxious to consummate lock and key, but
eventually must enter—no one home and
all that remains are my books, your bouquet
on the mantlepiece, and the ghostly footprints

etched in the carpet where furniture once rested,
so, I know it's here, the specter is with me still;
I pull the door tight as I follow my gray shadow inside
and shuffle after it, darkly, to bed.

DIFFERENTIAL CALCULUS FOR POETS

I wrote a poem for you
but never showed it because
its small truth was a line

weak and thin running
tangent to the great
curving Truth beneath it

LYING IN BED ONE EVENING

after you left
the California King reduced

in proportion and scale first to
Mississippi Prince then to

Alabama Duke and
at last

when it shrunk to become a
Carolina Vassal I

dragged the sheet into the den where
I dozed fitfully on the chair next to

the empty vase
in the dark of a kingdom

feudal and
without sovereignty

VELÁZQUEZ DREAMED OF YOU TAKING
SELFIES IN BED

He paid especial attention to the tufts of fabric:
chenille and cashmere piled
atop cotton and silk, and yet

the still gentler softness of you beneath it all,
white legs mingling with cream sheets,
the suggestion of curves under the blankets' folds

and you, luxuriating, studied your poses,
choosing among them the one evoking the least
artifice; then you bathed and breakfasted, and

studying the empty bedroom, the unmade bed,
felt suddenly uncertain about how to spend
the rest of your afternoon.

THE AIM OF ART

Those Chinese torturers knew: the
dripdrip dripdrip dripdrip dripdrip dripdrip
of the water against the chest erodes
capacity for thought until, at last, the victim

finds new clarity, accepts the trauma of this existence,
gives meaning to it upon discovering that the relentless
driving water has pickaxed a hole, felt though unseen,
through skin, bone, and tissue, boring down to a place

where a heart once beat and finding it filled
with something between
water and blood
soul and flesh

THE HEARTH

Shoveling ash from the fireplace
decades later, I remembered that back then
we never burned the Sunday funnies
but always crumbled the news, tucked the paper
under bits of kindling to start our fires—

my brother and I would strike the matches
just to smell the sulphur, and hide the lit
matchsticks among yesterday's news,
would fan the embers until they stoked
into flames; then, for a brief moment

would warm our backs before feeling
the bite of a cold, sharp wind
from the back door as our father,
shivering in his shirtsleeves, entered,
toting another armful of wood.

A WILLOW GROWS ASLANT A BROOK

The sheet draped water-thin, spread wide
from her shoulders
to her toes, curled under;

her face, lovely and lit by streetlamps,
strained the necks of passersby
as they tried to guess her name

but still she slept undisturbed—
the naloxone laid beside her, spent;
the breaths we saw, a trick

of the light.

BALLET IN THE PARK

ballet dancers glided past
as they performed *bourrées*
in the ethereal summer gloaming, their stage
set in the corner of the park,
watched by spectators who laid on a
patchwork of quilts across the grassy lawn
while hidden among the magnolias,

a chorus of cicadas counted the time,
out-singing Wagner as Isolde took the stage,
her face a crescent of moonlight, waning
        Gibbous, a
spinning infant's mobile, unknowable after a
        dozen wild
fouettés, until she stopped, resumed a
        classical pose and
stood, washed in the night's milky starlight.

I walked home before the third act,
my hands stuffed in empty pockets,
the sweetness of hunger on my breath,
and humming all the while a tune
whose words I did not know.

AFTER A LONG WALK

I came to your home
unannounced
empty-handed and

you received me by warming
the morning's pot of coffee
and buttering cold

biscuits

EVERY LEAF A FLOWER

We weren't lost
so much as stuck
in the county's
largest corn maze

until a child came
to show us the way free;
we walked back to the car
across the orchard, picked clean,

each of us on a row, ducking under the
branches in the stand of apple trees between us—
our hands dropped, raised as fingertips
brushed together between each new tree.

NUDE DESCENDING A STAIRCASE NO. 2

You know the feeling
the sound the sweetness

the pin-pricking heat playing
on the back of your neck

so let's not ruin the secret
of the heart

with words that cannot capture
what your soul already knows

only say that
when you see her

descend
you pause,

time arrests

CAFÉ AU COGNAC

Here is my trinity:
coffee, cognac, and cream—
where bitter, hot, and stout cut
through cold, and thick, and sweet;

find me during those nights
when I'm in need of strength
sitting at my table,
saying a prayer, taking a drink.

OF AN OCTOBER EVENING

Did you see the peach-
colored sun stretch oblate
at the horizon? The treetops

turned greenblack against it
when an autumn coolness fell—
and then night,

and then others of us, too.

STILL LIFE, NO. 2

The dying hydrangeas,
once the color of cream,
languished in the vase,

though the baby's breath
had another week of life
in them yet

EN PLEIN AIR

Did Constable paint the clouds?
Cézanne the rivers?
Rembrandt the sea?
Did Monet paint the fields of poppy

we're standing in, or is it simply that my
world seems more artfully wrought
with you in it? Each moment
is a painting hung in the galleries

of my fading memory.

PALM SUNDAY

Wisteria drop their petals
along the garden path

which mute our steps
as you and I walk

in the orange light of dusk.
Our hands lace together—

twisting vines on a trellis—
and I begin to tell you about the beauty

of this thought
but do not speak when I see your

reverence for it all, so on
we walk through the nave

of this open-air cathedral to
universal peace.

AUS DEM LEBEN DER BIENEN*

The bees have a language
worth hearing—though silent,

they dance, words in pirouettes,
waggling for the foragers

who don't know the way,
a dance to find the flowers, sweetly

hidden among a cruel,
interminable earth;

and as you swatted one away
that sat for a moment

on your glistening skin
I imagined the bee dancing tumbling drunk

for the hive, saying in words
not meant for human understanding

let me show you
how sweet she tastes

let me show you
the way

* "The Dancing Bees"

COCKAIGNE

She was old enough
to have had dreams
that could never be:

old enough to know
the subtle difference
between possibly and

probably; though that
truth never kept her from
believing in the beauty

of rough-hewn things,
like her hands, caked
from digging the garden

and the edges of her eyes,
crinkle-cut from years of
laughing with friends—

she sloughed away her dashed
expectations and learned
to prefer pulling

the radishes from her garden
and humming quiet hymns
while wandering the

white-fenced paths
that meandered to those
long-forgotten places

where she'd always been.

VAN GOGH DREAMED OF YOU WEARING LILLY PULITZER

You put on the dress with nowhere
particular to go since

the account was empty
the cards all maxed

but still you danced
in the sunflower fields of your soul

imagining a life where
the pearls that kissed your collarbones

were real.

PARADISO

Heaven must be in thee before thou canst be in Heaven.
—Geo. Swinnock

Whitman—take your multitudes
I have no need of them, since
there is Heaven inside me

cumulus clouds hang aloft my soul:
enter here, through eyes or lips or ears
stand on the cusp and see the open skies, verdant
    fields

where I picnic lazily and joyfully
where I walk often and work never at all
where I come to love those whom I am yet to love

no multitude exists here:
I am one; inside me is a place
that is one.

BERRY-PICKING WITH MY BROTHER: A SONNET

Thorns pricked our fingers
as we gathered blackberries
in the brambles beneath
the disused feed silo where

we dropped clumps of swollen fruit
into a white bucket until it stained
as purple or purplish red as our own hands,
yours a little larger, a little more purple than mine;

until the sun fell away into the pines and Grandpa
    called
us back, saying it's too dark here for children, so
    we trudged across
the field with the bucket swinging heavy between
    us, weighted
by the gravity of an ethic you could've shouldered
    on your own.

Grannie would use what she found in the bucket
    to can jam or
preserves, but not before Grandpa inspected
    them by
tasting the biggest, juiciest berries
and rewarding our job well done

by sneaking us ice cream sandwiches to eat in the
    dark
while Grannie put in her curlers before bed.

HARVEY

the yachts rocked in their slips
moored to the docks, helpless,
if a vessel can be such a thing,
while darkened sky and
heightened wind
eddied the clouds above them in
something like Prospero's tempest

but all settled, quieted, and
it seemed that the thing would
come stillborn, labor pangs just to
birth air, dust and some-
thing approximating flesh—
then fell the first drops, and the people
heard the newborn bitch begin to cry

A CARTOGRAPHER MAPS THE GEOGRAPHY
OF HOPE

Peanuts sloshed in the old man's cola
when he swigged it in gulps and surveyed
the desk before him, cluttered as it was
with the detritus of a lifetime:

ceramics from his travels and pens
received as gifts packed tightly
in a coffee cup; yet he held the pencil

worn thin and erased down to the ferrule,
the metal of it tapping on the worn desk, keeping time
while he stared at the blank paper, centered

in a space of emptiness carved out of the untidy
oak. He took the pencil, whose temporary
marks he could not erase, and began to write
to a person he once knew, address unknown.

ON A LONESOME EVENING

I left the market with
an armful of peonies and
a bottle of wine and strolled aimless
through the square for an hour after;

the bouquet's subtle headiness trailed behind me
in aromatic wakes and ripples while I
hoped that someone would see and believe
that I had somewhere to go, somebody to see.

FRAN LEBOWITZ BUMS A CIGARETTE

You're not from New York, she says
when I hand her the pack,

but maybe you live in Flatbush or Hoboken
if I had to guess—

I tell her no I am from Texas
but once for a year or two lived in Kentucky

near a horse farm
which, geographically,

is as close to living
in The City

as I ever got
if that counts for anything

to which she smiles coyly and says
just light it for me already

and the Marlboro I give her is
key money

well spent
to rent a studio in her

spacious Manhattan soul

YOUR HIGH SCHOOL LOVE LEAVES FOR COLLEGE

As you watch her leave
the diner, you sit alone
and you wonder
whether she will remember
you—and after she has left,
you remember the words you read
together in your literature class, the words
from a scholar of Dickinson who wrote that
the poet eschewed periods
because she could not stand

the spurious finality of a full stop,
and so it is in your heart:
you would prefer this love
to drift into nothingness than end
for isn't your love unendingly strong
and loyal and worthy
and damn it, and damn it, and damn it
aren't you worthy of love,
worthy of being
loved, and yet—

ON A VINEYARD TERRACE

A woman apologizes
to her friend upon hearing the news
of her recent divorce;

she replies
don't worry I'll be
okay
anyway honey try
the Syrah
some wines sing notes but
this one
melodies

WHEN THE BRIGHT BRING NONE

a telephone wire
bifurcated the sky
into above and below
between deep blue and deeper

but the lone drifting cloud took no notice
of these fine distinctions
and blew—claiming all—the airy pilgrim
sought other skies

other heavens

STILL LIFE, NO. 3

Under the desk lamp shone
a glass bottle of cola, quarter drunk, a pen
knife lodged in a half block of gruyere
and an open chicken-scratched journal
with all the lines crossed out

STANDING AT THE FOUNT

I stood shoulder to shoulder
with the bishop, an arrogant pisser—
he aimed straight for the water,
splashing loud—

but I, gun shy, pissed silent
against the side of the bowl;
made sure to wash my hands
thoroughly after.

PRAYER TO A SPARROW

For F. G. Lorca

Unearth the buried
sun with your beak

and give me light
so I may see what good

things grow beneath
the life-sustaining dawn.

IN A GARDEN

Hummingbirds skirt about
their feeders

instinct gives them fear and
hunger boldness

they flit nervously
as though

new lovers learning
the rhythms

of each other's bodies
hips tangling

the dance out of step
her arrhythmia

is his metronome
and yet

the thrill of synchrony
is sweet

so dance through the air
hummingbirds, lovers

BLOOMING

ice burned the ground
after a cruel winter—worst
in years, the old-timers said—

nonetheless, I found no serene
blankets of snow draping silence
over the firs, the pines, only ice

that stalled engines and broke hips,
ice that hung sharply from the eaves, ice
that fell, stabbing at the cold, hard earth;

finally, though,
sleet turned to hail,
hail to rain, then,

here, I saw the first sign of life:
among ice and slush and mud,
hungrily,

a doe ate
the as yet unbloomed
buds of spring

VALETTE DREAMED OF YOU ON
A RAINY STREET

you turned to face him
the moment before the driver
brought your car around—

you felt the shocks
of hair soaked through and streaking
your back while the arches
of your bare feet sunk into
the sidewalk; red-bottomed heels
dangled haphazard from your fingers
as you turned without speaking when

he called out for you
to wait, but whether waking or
sleeping, an unsettling haze descended;
the street blended into nothing but muted tones,
a morass of ambiguity
that aroused an anxious light-headedness
in him as he, disoriented, imagined a
        concordance

of all the unsaid words that would never
pass from your lips while you slipped away
into the fog of misremembered dreams

THE UNBEARABLE SILENCE OF GOD

from the empty orchestra
pit

a child plays
out of time

a half measure on the timpani
and abruptly quits

the stage

THE WITCH OF EAST TEXAS

We children believed her a witch.
Some adults, too, thought her
something from the Woods,

when they found her wandering
her lawn in the wee hours when, she thought,
no one could see, but more often we found her

peering a single eye between slats
of venetian blinds, held open by two
thin, aged fingers drenched in shadow—

my eye caught hers once
and held her gaze for a moment
before the slat of her blind

guillotined the light,
so I cycled on, unsteady,
in the fullness of the sun.

WEST, TEXAS

under smoky sky
glowing foundry red

the corrugated metal marries
rods of wrought iron

in the twisted decay, the wreckage
a crater of ruin, the rust on the tankers

sandblasted clean, bleached white
as mangled bones and

among the steel is flesh:
a father and infant son unmoving

in a pickup truck ditched on the farm-to-market
while, between them, mother, wife

daisy-chains grief to grief

THIS HORROR WILL GROW MILD

His sneakers played at the flecked lines
in the white linoleum floor
polished to a sterile mirror finish
though he didn't see his face in it,

even with head hung low, almost to his elbows;
an orderly came to ask if he needed water
while he waited, and yes, a drop before his expulsion
from Purgatory to another place would do fine, though

he didn't know what a poor consolation
it was until the doctor arrived,
rested a weary arm on his shoulder, and
wore a stoic look on his face.

THREE KINDS OF WISDOM

When I was young
I spent my money on books

in middle life
on wine

and now
on flowers.

SUBURBAN DAWN, AUTUMN

some stars are visible here—
between the last bar closing
and the first café opening—
but no one is out to see them
tonight, until Venus, alone, rises
in the East, as sprinklers turn on
and coffee begins to percolate
in ten thousand coffeepots;

all the while, in woods
behind the brick walls,
Morningstar gives way
to Daystar, and
a barn owl leaps
from its branch and
snatches a crying hare
in its talons

ADVICE TO MY NEPHEW

For John Thomas, on the occasion of his
    first birthday

don't make the same mistakes I did,
but by all means, make mistakes, so:

tell dirty jokes, swear,
drink whiskey, wine, and beer

smoke tobacco, chase women
cause trouble and give your parents hell;

if you do these things and are right and
    honest and true
then at the very least you'll have a good
    story.

But above all, remember: It's *your* story.

A LESSON IN KARATE

don't punch the board
but just past it
land square in the space
behind the plank

where the air is—
that's the trick:
aim for the emptiness
and you will punch through

the hard stuff

ON A GAS STATION CURB

The lady's eyes—
hidden in a wetly
red, puffy face—

darted through
the half-inch sheaf
of lottery tickets,

searching for
something like
hope

but finding
something
else instead.

STILL LIFE, NO. 4

precariously on the tub's ledge
rest a stoneware mug of coffee,
hotter than the bath, and a spoon
propped against the china creamer

dish on the tray with strawberry wafers,
while the funny pages, already read, lay
wilting on the wet tile floor

RETROGRADE

in the city
all the stars
were airplanes

forming constellations
of untold
mythologies

NOT ALL GOOD THINGS HARMONIZE

not all notes strike a chord
nor all chords produce a melody

so why should you, why should I
harmonize?

but there's beauty, sometimes,
in singing a song

a little off-key
out of tune

and enjoying the lyrics sloshing out
haphazard from a well in your soul

it's true: not all good things
harmonize, but sometimes,

sometimes
they do

PARADISE REGAINED

I did not have the heart
to kill

the snake in my garden
so I called out

to my neighbor
who came with a spade.

CODA

she blows against
a cupped hand
and the votive flickers out,

the wisps of smoke—
invisible in the new dark—
disperse, extinguish unseen

my eyes,
unacclimated,
shift, searching for

a memory of light—
it was here
it was just here

Arise, shine; for thy light is come.

ISAIAH 60:1